21 METAPHYSICAL SECRETS

Life Changing Truths For Unconventional Thinkers

Including 9 Do-It-Yourself Energy Experiments

Inhalt

Introduction

There is a famous Indian fable where six blind men come across an elephant. The first blind man feels its massive side and tells the others that an elephant is like a wall. The second blind man feels the elephant's tusk and reports to the others that an elephant is like a spear. The third blind man encounter's the elephant's trunk and informs the others that an elephant is like a snake. The fourth blind man feels the leg of the elephant and reports that an elephant is like a tree. The fifth blind man encounters the elephant's ear and indicates to the others that an elephant is like a fan. The sixth blind man touches the elephant's tail and states that an elephant is like a rope.

The fable of the blind men and the elephant is a metaphor for how we experience reality. What we refer to as "reality" or the "real world" is based on our sensory abilities, our socialization, and our beliefs. Based on these factors, we believe that our experience of reality is the "true" reality. Each of the blind men in the fable had an experience with the elephant and came away from it with a partial truth; however, the truth of the elephant was missed by all of them. By relying on our beliefs and limited sensory acuity, our perception of reality can be distorted, just as with the blind men.

All conflict among our species is the result of us experiencing life differently. Each person's experience of life is unique, and each person believes that they are experiencing the "real world." There is no challenge that we can face, individually or collectively, that we cannot transcend by changing our perspective. The higher the level of awareness we achieve, the more perspectives that we apply to our lives.

When we can live from different perspectives, we experience greater happiness and freedom. We are not confined to the narrow band of experiences by which most of humanity lives their lives. The purpose of this book is to expose you to different perspectives. By opening yourself up to these different perspectives, you can cultivate a deeper awareness of the nature of reality as well as apply them to your life in a practical way.

When we can embrace the so-called metaphysical world and the "real world," we become intentional participants in the evolution of the human species. The "evolution" that I speak of is the evolution of consciousness, which is the ultimate expression of love.

What is Metaphysics?

Metaphysics is the philosophy that deals with the origin, or the first principle, of all that we experience. It deals with the non-phenomenal aspect of life. The word non-phenomenal refers to something that cannot be perceived through our five senses. Given this, metaphysics explains the appearance of that which is phenomenal, that which is perceivable by our five senses.

There is a metaphysical component to every aspect of our lives. The question is are we aware of it? Extra Sensory Perception (ESP) is a metaphysical topic that many in the scientific community do not take seriously. However, the concept of time is a subject of interest for both meta-physicists and physicists. Why is ESP not treated with the same level of interest as time is? It is because we all experience time, even though time is non-phenomenal. The same cannot be said of ESP. Many people do not believe in ESP or do not believe that they can perceive the extra sensory. What prevents us from experiencing the metaphysical is our beliefs.

The gulf between metaphysics and traditional science is beginning to narrow with the advent of quantum physics. Scientists are now discovering behaviors of the atomic world that go against everything we know in our physical world. Rather than choosing sides between the metaphysical and scientific, more and more researchers are incorporating both as they seek to find the answers to those larger questions that humanity has always pondered.

21 Metaphysical Secrets

The Nature of your Being and Existence

Do you exist? Anyone who is asked this question would give an instant and unqualified "yes!" How is it that we can answer this question without any sense of doubt? We can do so because we are aware of our existence. Because we are aware of our existence, we are also aware of the existence of all that we experience. How do you know you exist? What is your answer to this question? Regardless of what your answer is, you are aware of your answer as well! That aspect of you that is aware of your existence and your experiences is your being.

Throughout your life, you have had innumerable experiences, and all of them have involved change. You experienced change in your thoughts and beliefs. You have experienced change in your emotions and feelings. You have experienced change in your perceptions, and you have experienced change in your physical body. You have also experienced change in your surroundings. During the night, you experienced altered states of consciousness that gave rise to dreaming and deep sleep. You have experienced all of these changes; however, there is one constant. This constant has never changed. That constant is your awareness.

Everything that you experience occurs within the field of awareness, including that which you experience as being "you." That which we refer to as "awareness" is the fundamental nature of who you are.

Your being cannot be perceived through your senses or conceived by your mind; it can only be known intuitively. Anything that exists within awareness is what we refer to as experience. The existence of anything is the validation of the awareness of it. That which is aware is the nature of your being.

When speaking about consciousness, it easy to misinterpret what it is. No description will ever be given that captures the nature of consciousness because consciousness is beyond what the mind can understand. To help minimize the potential for confusion, let us replace the word "consciousness" with "knowing."

For knowing to exist, there needs to be three elements: The knower, the object that is known, and the knowing of the object. Let us use an example to illustrate this. I know that there is a tree in my yard. I (the knower) knows (the knowing of) there is a tree (the object).

Is it possible for me to separate the "knowing of" (also known as awareness) from the object of my awareness (the tree)? Determine this for yourself by looking at an object. Is the knowing of the object inseparable from the object itself? Of course, it is! The knowing of any object and the object that is known are inseparable from each other.

The knowing of your own existence is inseparable from existence itself. Thus,
your sense of self is an object of a greater knowing. Who or what has a knowing of you? Can you separate that which knows of you from the object that is you? That which knows of my own existence, can I separate it from the knowing that I have of the tree?

That which I refer to as "I," and my knowing of the tree, and the tree itself, are one in the same. That which knows of "I," and my knowing of the tree, and the tree itself, are also one in the same. Ultimately, all that there is knowing, or as I have used in this book, consciousness. You are an aspect of a greater consciousness.

For there to be a knowing of, there must be a knower and the object that is known. For pure consciousness to know anything, it must have an object to know. It is for this purpose that consciousness expresses itself in manifested from. You and I are an example of this manifestation.

For us to serve pure consciousness, it is necessary for us to take on physical form and a sense of individuality, or

"I."   It is this sense of "I," along with our identification with our physical form that creates a sense of separation from all the other forms of manifestation.

It is our sense of contrast between ourselves and other manifestations that creates new potentialities, which we know as thought. It is thought that creates our sense of experience and informs the pure or greater consciousness of its own nature.   In response to our thoughts, the pure consciousness creates new potentialities that are consistent with the information that it has received from us.

What we refer to as consciousness is actually a consciousness system. You and I are localized aspects of the greater consciousness that are generating experiences for the larger consciousness system. Since we, localized consciousness, are inseparable from the greater consciousness, you and I are both the source of all of our experiences as well the experiencers of it. Our experience is what we refer to as existence, while the nature of being is that which knows of existence.

Do-It-Yourself Energy Experiment:

All of our problems, without exception, are the result of personalizing our experiences. We personalize our experiences because we identify with the thought that we have of our selves. By practice the exercise under the topic: Ego and Identity, you can recondition your mind to become an observer of your experiences, rather than personalizing them. The benefits of this will be greater peace, greater calm, expanded awareness, and diminishing judgmental thinking.

Nature of Reality: What is it?

In discussing *Existence and the Nature of Being,* we discussed that our essential being is awareness and that we know of existence because we are aware of it. Given the essential nature of our being is awareness, every living being is actually just one being.

If there is an awareness of that which you refer to as "you," and every other living being also has a sense of itself, then the essential aspect of all beings is the same awareness. Ultimately, all that there is awareness or consciousness. The nature of the world of form that we experience is the unlimited expressions of consciousness being projected through thought.

When dreaming, you experience yourself as a character that inhabits a dream world. This dream world seems so real that you do not realize it is just a dream until you wake up. Your dream self is fully engaged with its dream world. All of your senses are functioning. You can have thoughts, make plans, and take action.

As real as your dream experience may be, it is illusionary. Both your dream self and its dream world are the projections of your own consciousness. Just as you are the creator of your dream experience, universal consciousness expresses itself as individuated or localized forms of consciousness. These individuated expressions of consciousness experience themselves as being separate from the other localized expressions of consciousness. You and I are the localized expressions of the greater consciousness. Just as in the dream, we project our experiences which become our experience of reality.

There is no one objective reality; rather, each expression of consciousness is creating their own unique and subjective sense of reality, though there are some experiences that are part of the collective consciousness. It is for this reason that we all experience a "world" outside of ourselves; yet, that "world" will be experienced differently by each person.

Do-It-Yourself Energy Experiment:

Practice suspending judgment and the need to be right. Also, practice letting go of the need to be certain about what things mean. Doing both of these things will allow you to experience going beyond your sense of certainty and experience a perspective that you may have never experienced before. It will increase your sense of creativity and compassion.

The Things that We do: Determinism versus Free Will

What is the origin of your behaviors? Do you freely choose your behaviors, or are your behaviors the results of factors outside of yourself? Determinism is the school of thought that governs most of the sciences and many schools of psychology. An example would be B. F. Skinner who conditioned a dog to salivate after repeatedly presenting a piece of meat while ringing a bell at the same time. Before the dog learned to associate the meat with the bell, it would salivate just by seeing the meat. After the dog learned to associate the sound of the bell with the meat, it salivated just from hearing the sound of the bell.

Imagine that you are on the freeway driving over the speed limit, until you see a police car following you. The sight of the police car causes you to adjust your speed. The salivating of the dog and the adjustment of your speed were both the effects of environmental factors, namely the bell and the police officer.

As opposed to determinism, the concept of free will states that our behaviors are a product of our free choice, that we choose our behavior rather than our behavior being the result of some environmental factor.

The challenge posed by the concepts of determinism and free will is that they are both the product of our rational mind. The mind is only able to understand the phenomenal world, meaning that which can be detected by the senses or through the experience of thought. The mind is unable to detect the non-phenomenal. How we perceive that which we refer to as the self can make a big difference as to whether we see our actions as being the result of external factors or from free will.

If we see ourselves as being a distinct, physical entity that lives in a world populated by objects and other physical beings, then determinism would seem to make sense. By seeing ourselves as distinct, physical entities, everything that we experience will be perceived as being separate from ourselves. I see the furniture in my home or my family members as being separate entities from myself because I see myself as a separate being unto myself. It would make sense that my behaviors are the result of my interactions with these and other entities. An argument could also be made that some of my behaviors can also spring from free choice. My wife may ask me to do a certain task. My handling the task for her would seem to fit the model of determinism. However, I have the free will to schedule my doing of the task when it would work best for both of us. So, is my behavior a product of determinism, free-will, or both?

Do you have control of your thoughts? How long can you go without having a thought? Do you have control over the sensations that you experience? Can you control the rate at which your body ages? Can you control the flow of your blood or the metabolism of your body? The deeper that we look into our lives, the more that we see that so much of our life is not in our control. We cannot control our dreams, nor can we control the length of our life span.

If you have ever practiced meditation at a deep enough level, it is indisputable that we have an awareness of all of our experiences. We experience the world through the five senses, and we have an awareness of our perceptions, our sensations, the sounds that we hear, and that which we taste. If we are aware of all of these forms of sensory input, then we cannot be our experiences, including our experience of the body and thought.

As we are aware of the physical body and our mental functions, who we are, at the deepest level, cannot be the physical body or our mental functions. That which is awareness, is it subject to determinism or free will? How can awareness be subject to determinism or free will when all of experience is dependent on the awareness of it? Awareness is ever present. Whether we are wide awake, dreaming, or in a deep sleep, there is an awareness of it. Determinism and free will can only exist if there is an awareness of it.

If we see ourselves as a multidimensional being, that we are both phenomenal and non-phenomenal in nature, perhaps we can agree on one thing, we have the free-will to direct our focus and attention. Ultimately, that may be the only thing that we are in control of.

In western society, we have been socialized to believe that the world is divided into an inner and the outer realms. We directly experience our thoughts, perceptions, and sensation, all of which we refer to as aspects of ourselves. These things are considered to be our inner realm. The objects of our thoughts, perceptions, and sensations are experienced as our outer realm.

We experience the world through our five senses and make sense of it through our thoughts. We equate our thoughts to the "mind." No one has ever seen a "mind," though we have been socialized to believe that we have one. On the other hand, everything that we experience with our five senses can be known as it has a physical reality to it. It can be measured, weighed, touched, and so on. It is from this separation of these two realms that we come up with concepts such as "mind over matter" or "mind and matter."

The divide between mind and matter is an illusion, an illusion created by thought. The reason why the ancient practice of meditation remains thriving today is that the illusion of separation between mind and body cannot hold up to deeper inspection.

Try this simple experiment. If you are experienced in meditation, get into a relaxed meditative state. If you are inexperienced in meditation, simply close your eyes and relax. Avoid engaging with your thoughts by simply accepting everything that you experience without judgment or trying to control anything.

As the activity of your mind starts to slow down, place your attention on your thoughts. That you can pay attention to your thoughts demonstrates that your thoughts can be perceived by you; you have a knowing of their existence. Now place your attention on the chair or the floor that you are sitting on. You are aware of the sensations that arise from that which you are sitting on it.

The chair or the floor that you are sitting on, according to our socialization and conditioning, is made of matter. As you experience sensations of the surface that you are sitting on, you experience it as being something outside of yourself (unlike thought). Also, the surface that you are sitting on has volume and mass (unlike thought). Both thought and the surface that you are sitting on are recognized by you through awareness. You are aware of the movement of thought, and you are aware of the sensations of the surface.

Now go back into your meditation and determine for yourself as to whether you can separate your awareness of thought from the thought itself. Can you separate the awareness of the sensation of the surface from the surface itself?

The awareness of anything is inseparable from that which you are aware of. How can mind and matter be separate when both thought and the surface are inseparable from awareness?

Mind and matter are but properties of our conceptual thinking. It is our limited perception that leads us to believe that they are of separate realities.

Do-It-Yourself Energy Experiment:

Practice the exercise, described in this topic, until you experience yourself as no longer begin separate from the world around you. You will know that you have reached this level of awareness when your experience of yourself seems to merge with that which you are observing, which is the essence of love. The benefits of this exercise are that you will recondition your mind so that your sense of connection with life will be enhanced.

Under the topic of *Mind and Matter*, you were guided to the discovery that mind and matter are not separate, that they are both manifestations of consciousness. Anything that we attribute to being an aspect of the mind or matter is also a manifestation of consciousness. Given this, even your sense of self and your physical body is a manifestation as well. The universe that we experience is not something that exists outside of us. Rather, the universe that we experience is a manifestation of consciousness and is projected from within us.

The Law of Attraction has received much attention since the release of the 2006 bestseller, the *Secret*. The theme of the book is that you manifest your world and that you can attract that which you desire with your thoughts. Whether you believe in the Law of Attraction or not is irrelevant when viewed from the perspective of higher awareness. The reason for this is that everyone is attracting their experiences of life, whether they are conscious of it or not. After all, the essence of who we are is inseparable from the rest of life. If you believe in the Law of Attraction and are practicing it, then you are consciously manifesting in your life as opposed to manifesting unconsciously. This is the only difference between believing in the Law of Attraction and not believing in it.

Like everything else in life, how we experience happiness is dependent upon our level of conscious awareness. For most of humanity, happiness is experienced as an emotion when an unfulfilled desire is met. A person who is unhappy because they feel lonely may become happy upon starting a relationship with someone new. Similarly, a person may be struggling financially and then become happy upon receiving a large sum of money. In either case, the happiness that is experienced is contingent upon the circumstances of the person aligning with their desires.

When the person's circumstances do not align with their desires, their happiness will fade. The person who found a new relationship may later get their feelings hurt by the other person. The person who received a large sum of money may discover that they are responsible for paying a large tax bill. Because happiness, for most of us, is based on external conditions, our happiness is transitory.

For others, especially, in the spiritual community, happiness is sought not in their external conditions but from within. Perhaps they believe in God, or some universal power. Because their focus is not on external conditions, their sense of happiness may seem more stable. However, even this experience of happiness has its pitfalls.

When people who are following a spiritual path feel happy, they reinforce the belief that it is their spiritual path that is making them happy. However, there will be times when they feel unhappy. At such times, they may resist the feelings of unhappiness because they may feel that they should not feel that way. This resistance to experiencing unhappiness can lead to the person either blocking out their feelings or engage in self-doubt. There is another alternative, which is the understanding that happiness is something that cannot be pursued or gained. The nature of happiness is such that it arises when we stop searching for it.

There is an inherent peace that lies within the depths of us all. Its existence is independent of anything outside of us or any spiritual path. To unveil and realize this inner peace only requires inquiry into one's self.

When we establish our lives in this place, we can experience any emotion yet remain untouched by it. Whether it is the emotion of ecstasy or grief, the emotion is fully experienced; yet, a sense of peace and acceptance underlies it all. It is like a person who is watching a movie. During the movie, there may be scenes of sadness, conflict, hope, and victory. While the person may be caught up in the movie, he or she knows that it is just a movie.

When we establish inner peace within us, there is nothing that we can experience that will rob us of our peace, which cannot be said of happiness. How do we learn to establish inner peace? It is actually very simple. It is simple because there is nothing for us to establish! It is the very nature of our existence to be at peace. The reason why we do not experience peace is not because we have to gain anything; rather, we need to lose something. That something is our self-identification with our mind. The essence of who we are is the knower of thoughts, emotions, feelings, perceptions, and sensations. When we learn to observe them, without getting involved with them, we will reconnect with our sense of peace.

Do-It-Yourself Energy Experiment:

Learning to meditate is a great way to connect with the sense of peace described in this topic. Most meditations that are taught ask you to visualize a peaceful scene or to focus on something, like your breath. Instead, try meditating but do not focus on anything. Do not visualize or try to control anything. Allow yourself to experience whatever you are experiencing without trying to get involved with it. To quote a Beetles tune, "Let it Be."

Time is just an illusion. We experience linear time and believe it to be real. Einstein showed that time is relative and is part of a time-space continuum. Past and future are illusionary. Everything that has ever existed, or will exist, exists in the present. It is our mind that creates a sense of past and future. Our conditioning and beliefs affect our experience of time. The less we cling to our conditioning and beliefs, the more we will experience timelessness.

Our experience of time and space is based on our identifying with body and mind. We believe that the thoughts that we experience are our thoughts. We believe that the emotions and feelings that we experience are our emotions and feelings. We believe the body that we experience is our body. Anything that we experience that is apart from our minds and bodies is experience as being something separate from ourselves. Our sense of time and space is based on this sense of separation.

The deepest level of consciousness is pure consciousness, which is devoid of all thought or memory. The qualities of pure consciousness are oneness, wholeness, boundless, and eternal. Everything that exists, phenomenal or non-phenomenal, arises from pure consciousness; however, it is not separate from pure consciousness. To illustrate this, imagine a drop from the ocean. The drop is an expression of the ocean that has qualities that are vastly different from the ocean. The drop is of much smaller size, lacks the waves and currents of the ocean, nor does it harbor the abundance of marine life that the ocean does. However, its essential composition is no different than the ocean. The drop contains the same chemical composition as the ocean itself. If you return the drop to the ocean, it merges with it without any distinction.

Thought is a manifestation of pure consciousness. As with the drop and the ocean, thought has many qualities that are unique, but its essential nature is the same as pure consciousness. Unlike pure consciousness, thoughts can be perceived by our awareness. We know when we are experiencing a thought. Thoughts contain information (which we refer to as memory), while pure consciousness is devoid of information. Finally, thoughts are fleeting in their existence, unlike pure consciousness which is eternally present. Despite all these differences, the essential nature of thought is pure consciousness. Everything that we experience is pure consciousness appearing in an infinite variety of forms.

Thought is like a filter through which pure consciousness is converted into what we refer to as time and space. At the level of pure consciousness, time, distance, space, separation, variety, distinctions, boundaries, and limitations are non-existent. Thought is like a snap shot of pure consciousness while at the same time creating the impression of qualities that we experience as reality. Among those qualities are time and space.

There is no such thing as time and space. Time and space are the constructions of the mind that are projected on to our experience of reality. These constructs of the mind are like an image projected on a screen. The images of the movie comes from the projector and are projected on screen. If you turn off the projector, the screen would become blank. Similarly, if we let go of our attachment to our thoughts, we would not project them on that which we are experiencing.

What we experience as being time is the movement of thought. We may have one thought that tells us that the candle on our table is burning. Later, we may have the thought that the candle has burned down to half of its original size. We experience these changes as the passing of time. In fact, everything that has ever existed is occurring at the same time. We will discuss this in more detail under the topic of parallel universes.

Do-It-Yourself Energy Experiment:

You can change your experience of time if you learn to divert your attention away from your thoughts. Next time you do something that you enjoy, notice how the passage of time differs from when you are doing something that you do not enjoy. Normally, your experience of time speeds up when you are doing something you enjoy because you are more engaged with the task at hand. When doing a task that you do not enjoy, the passage of time tends to be slower because you are spending more time paying attention to your thoughts.

The truth of God cannot be experienced through the mind, nor can it be experienced through religion or some sacred texts. Even prayer, in most cases, is not directed toward God's truth. The reason for this is that any concept that we have of God is just that, a concept. A concept is a form of thought. How can a thought of "God" know the truth of God's existence? A thought cannot know anything; thought is just information. The awareness that knows of the existence of thought is more primal greater than thought itself.

By its very nature, the rational mind cannot conceive that which is non-phenomenal. Our minds can only detect the phenomenal, meaning that which we can perceive through our five senses and experience as thought. For most of humanity, the experience of God is contained within our thoughts, perceptions, feelings, or feelings. How else can we experience God? The challenge is that most of humanity identifies themselves with their mind and body. Any quality or characteristic that we give to our experience of God is the result of our own minds, not through the knowing of God.

As we discussed throughout this book, your fundamental nature is awareness or consciousness. Anything that you will ever experience is an object in the field of your awareness. The truth of who you are, the source of awareness, cannot be known by your conscious mind. The closest you will ever come to knowing your true self, in this lifetime, is in deep sleep. As stated earlier, deep sleep is devoid of thought and experience. We have no memory of deep sleep; yet, we are aware of the fact that it occurred. There could be no existence if there was no awareness of it. Pure consciousness, God, and your essential nature are one in the same.

The perspective that most of humanity holds is that we are a physical being that has a mind, from which thinking occurs. Because we experience ourselves as physical beings, we experience a sense of separation. As individual beings, we see ourselves as beings that are separate entities from all other physical forms. It is this sense of separation that creates our experience of time. It is our fixation on the world of form, along with illusions of time that leads us to believe that there is only one reality, the reality that we experience.

When viewed from the perspective of higher consciousness, that which we call reality is illusionary. From this perspective, time and separation do not exist. From this perspective, there are innumerable realities that are occurring all at the same time. To understand this, we first need to take a deeper look at the nature of energy and thought.

The fundamental ingredient of that which we refer to as the universe is energy and information. Everything that exists is made of energy, which has an innate intelligence to it. It is this intelligence that allows energy to take on multiple forms, which can be exemplified by the different phases that water can take on. Water can appear as a gas, liquid, or solid. What triggers a change in the phase that water takes on is temperature. The higher the temperature, the further apart are its water molecules. The lower the temperature, the closer the water molecules are to each other.

Molecules are composed of atoms, and over 90% of what constitutes an atom is energy. It is the information contained in energy that allows water to express itself in its various potentials. As time does not exist, other than a concept within our mind, all potentials exist at the same moment. Meaning, the potentials for water to be a liquid, solid, or gas can all exist at the same time. Given that we only experience one dimension of reality, it appears that the passage of time is required for water to change into its different phases.

It is only our conceptual mind that makes it appear that our experience of reality is the only reality. By learning to develop higher states of awareness, there is an infinite number of realities that we can experience. In our current reality, you are your current age. In another reality, you may be dead, while in another reality you have yet to be born.

The nature of reality is determined by our identification with thought. The less we cling to any given thought, the more open we will become to experience other realities or universes.

It is only at the level of ordinary awareness that we experience birth and death. As our fundamental nature is consciousness, our lives are eternal. The physical body is just an expression of consciousness, not the essence of who we are.

Everything in this life undergoes entropy, where the atomic particles of an object fluctuate between randomness and order. A metaphor for entropy would be the way water takes on different states. In its liquid form, water molecules have a lot of space between them, allowing them to move freely. This freedom of movement is why liquids can take on the shape of the space that it occupies. When water freezes, it becomes a solid, which we refer to as ice.

As ice, the water molecules are in direct contact with each other, offering little room for movement. When water is boiled, or evaporates, it becomes a gas. In its gas form, the water molecules have vast distances between them. Because of this, water loses all appearance of form or physicality.
In its solid state, the molecules have an order to them, while there is randomness in its gaseous state.

The water molecules themselves are composed of atoms, two hydrogen atoms, and one oxygen atom. While the atom was once considered a solid particle, we now know that this is just an illusion. The atom is actually made of subatomic particles separated from each other by vast distances of space. Even the subatomic particles lack any solidity to them as they are actually fluctuations of energy.

What we know as to be water is, at its most fundamental level, energy that takes on different configurations that result in it taking on different appearances, according to our perception.

We are no different than water in that we are also composed of atoms and molecules. Just as water takes on different states, we too take on different forms. Birth and death are the names that we have given to our experience of entropy. At the most fundamental level, there is no distinction between you, me, and this book that you are reading. Reincarnation is the name that we have given to the changing of entropy.

Most of us consider Extra Sensory Perception to be a special gift if we believe in it at all. One reason for this is the result of how we perceive ourselves and thought. We experience ourselves as distinct entities onto ourselves, separate from other people. We also believe that our thoughts are generated from our brains and that they are uniquely our own. As we ascend to higher level of consciousness, we begin to realize that any sense of separation is just an illusion. As for the origin of thoughts, how can we have our own thoughts when our sense of separation is just an illusion?

Thoughts are not generated by your mind; rather, you attract thoughts to you, which you experience as being yours.

Each one of us has the potential to experience any thought that has ever or will ever exist. The ability to tap into higher levels of consciousness is what we refer to as ESP, and any one of us can do it. What prevents some of us from realizing our ESP abilities are the beliefs that we hold on to. The following are examples of beliefs that prevent us from tapping into our ability for ESP:

- ESP is not real.
- I don't have ESP.
- ESP is a special ability.

Just as with experiencing parallel universes, the less that we identify with our thoughts, the greater we will be able to experience ESP.

The Awareness of Awareness: How Deep Can you Go?

Take a moment to look at your surroundings. Now place your attention on yourself. Having done so, answer these two questions: Are you are aware of your surroundings? Are you aware of yourself? The answer to both of these questions would be an immediate "yes"! Additionally, you are aware of thought, of the images that appear in your mind, and the sensations that you feel. Here is another question. Do you exist? The answer to that question would be another resounding "yes." You are aware of all of these things, but there is a more subtle level of awareness that you may not have ever considered: Are you aware of being aware?

Nothing can be experienced unless there is an awareness of it, even the most profound and subtlest forms of experience are detected by our awareness. Experience owes its existence to awareness.

When sleeping, we go through different levels of sleep. At the first level of sleep, we redirect our attention from the outer world and focus on the internal world. At this stage, we still have a strong identification with our physical body and mind. In the dream state, our sense of identification with the body greatly diminishes, and our awareness is heightened, allowing us to experience our subconscious thoughts and memories. We call these subconscious thoughts and memories "dreams." In deep sleep, we lose all sense of identification with our physical body and mind as our awareness retreats further within.

In deep sleep, we return to the source of awareness itself, pure consciousness. Pure consciousness is devoid of all thoughts or memory. It is for this reason that you are unable to remember your experience of deep sleep. For there to be an experience, there must be a memory of it. There can be no memory without thought, which is why we are unable to recall our experience of deep sleep. Despite this fact, we know that we experienced deep sleep. How can that be? While we have no memory of deep sleep, we still had an awareness of it. You have an awareness of that which is beyond thought or memory! The reason why you have an awareness of deep sleep is because who you are at the most fundamental level is awareness itself. At your most essential form, you are the awareness of deep sleep, dreams, your mind, your physical body, and everything else that you experience. You are awareness that is aware of itself.

What is your Purpose?

As long as we experience ourselves as purely physical beings separate from the rest of life, we will feel the need for a sense of purpose. The need for a sense of purpose is real and having a sense of purpose can powerfully impact our lives. On the other hand, having a lack of purpose can also lead to a sense of being disconnected from others and feeling that our lives have no meaning.

The idea of a life purpose is the sole property of the mind. Nowhere but in the human species does the purpose of life become an issue. Nature functions beautifully without pondering life's purpose.

The greater we elevate our consciousness awareness, the less necessary a life's purpose will be needed. Consider the state of deep sleep. Who among us does not enjoy the experience of waking up in the morning after spending the night in deep sleep? During deep sleep, did you worry about your purpose in life? Yet, you woke up feeling fresh and renewed. The need for a purpose in life is the product of the ego. This is not to say that having a sense of purpose is not necessary; it is as long as we are controlled by the ego. The key thing to ask one's self is "Am I happy?" If not having a sense of purpose is making you unhappy, then it may be something that is worthwhile to explore. If you can be happy without a sense of purpose, a sense of purpose is not needed.

When pursuing one's life purpose, three misunderstandings make it difficult to identify one's life purpose. The first misunderstanding is that one's life purpose must be something of grand scale or that it will impact the world. In truth, one's life purpose could be as simple being a better parent or doing volunteer work in the community. To better understand this, if a person's search for life's purpose is driven by the ego, that person is really being driven by the need to feel significant. Such a person will focus on those things that will be more grandiose and which will put them in the spotlight. In contrast, consider someone who gets involved doing volunteer work in their community out of the desire to contribute. Because they enjoy what they are doing, they will more likely be led to their life purpose.

The main thing is not to spend time pondering your life purpose; rather, expose yourself to new situations and be aware of those situations that resonate with you. Your feelings for a situation are more reliable in identifying your life's purpose than is your rational thinking.

Do-It-Yourself Energy Experiment:

The following are guidelines for finding your purpose:
1. Stop thinking about your life's purpose and start exposing yourself to new experiences. That which resonates with you will align with your purpose.

2. Make a list of all the things that you enjoy doing.
3. Make a list of all of your strengths and abilities.
4. Identify a need that others have.
5. Determine how you could apply steps 2 and 3 to fulfill the need in step 4.

As discussed in the topic on reincarnation, the essence of your life is eternal. As a species that is deeply attached to our conceptual thinking, we experience birth and death as the expression of new life and the loss of existing life. From the perspective of higher awareness, there is no new life or loss of existing life; there is only life. What we refer to as life and death are just two sides of the same coin. Birth and death are our perceptions and conceptual understandings of an eternal life force that is constantly creating new configurations of expression.

You experience things, but who or what is experiencing you? And that which experiences you, can it be experienced? Here is a simple exercise for inquiring on the nature of you.

1. Take a moment to relax and then look around your surroundings.
2. Pick an object in your environment and place your attention on it.

Now that you have done this, I have a question for you: What was the object that you were looking at? However you answer this question, your answer was formulated as a thought. If your answer to this question was that you were observing a tree, that answer was experienced as a thought. If you were observing a tree, then that was a perception. You had a perception and a thought of a tree.

My next question for you is how do you know that you had a perception and a thought of a tree? You knew you had a perception and a thought because there was awareness of it. There can be no experience without the awareness of it. Both "thought," "perception," and "tree" are concepts that we learned about when we were young. We can never know anything about "thought," "perception," or "tree." Can you touch, feel, measure, or observe a concept? Of course, you can't. We can only know the existence of them.

As you grew up, you learned about different concepts, and you started associating them to your experience. As a certain age, you replaced your pure experience of the world with concepts of it. As an infant, my experience of a tree was pure, unfiltered by the concepts that I had yet to learn. That changed when I started gaining information from those around me. Anything that I learned about trees, from that point on, became another concept that was combined with the existing concepts that I had of trees.
Today, I can name different species of trees. I can tell you of their size, their color, or their shape. Concepts are useful when communicating information about trees, but they can never take the place of the tree. Concepts are just a form of thought. I can think of a "tree"; I can hold concepts of a "tree," and I can perceive a "tree," but none of these are the tree itself

My thoughts and perceptions of a "tree" are like the experiences of the blind men and the elephant. Just as they never could experience the truth of the elephant, my thoughts and perceptions can never know the truth of a tree. All that I can ever know of a tree are my thoughts and perceptions of it. This is not just true of the tree; it is true for all of experience.

We can never know anything about our experiences other than our awareness of them. Any meaning we give to our experiences is a product of our thoughts. That which we experience has no inherent meaning; we create the meaning of our experiences. Who you are at your most essential level is the one who creates experiences and gives meaning to it; yet, your essential being is untouched by any experience. A light that shines on water illuminates the water; however, the light never becomes wet. You are the awareness of all experience, yet no experience can touch awareness.

Do-It-Yourself Energy Experiment:

Learning to not hold on to your conceptual thinking is a great way to experience expanded awareness. While concepts come in handy when communicating information, clinging to them create boundaries to our ability to experience. The reason for this is that we are focusing on our concepts, which prevent us from considering what lies beyond them. Besides meditation, the following is another way to practice perceiving without resorting to concepts:

1. Sit down and make yourself comfortable.
2. Take a few minutes to scan your environment, observing the people, plants, animals, or objects that are within your vicinity.

Now close your eyes and imagine that you are from another planet and have been sent to planet Earth to gather information about it. Being that you are from outer space, you have no previous knowledge or experience of Earth. You are like a newborn baby seeing the world for the first time.

Now open your eyes and look around again as you did the first time, remembering not to interpret, label, or judge anything that you see. Observe as though you were a blank slate.

Did your second observation have a different quality to it as compared to your first observation? Many people report that their second observation seemed fresh and more vibrant, that they felt more connected to life and themselves, that they felt more peaceful. If you were unable to detect a difference between the two observations, continue to practice until you can discern a difference.

As discussed previously in this book, we do not have thoughts; we do not generate thoughts from our brain. In other words, your thoughts are not yours! We have been socialized to believe that our thoughts belong to us because we have developed a deep identification with mind and body. In fact, there is no such thing as a "mind." What we refer to as "mind" is just a thought.

We previously discussed that deep sleep is devoid of thought as deep sleep is really the experience of pure consciousness. What we refer to as thought is a manifestation of the pure consciousness. There are various gradations of manifestation of the pure consciousness. The manifestations of consciousness appear in gradations of physicality. At one end of the spectrum are those things that we know as light and thought. Both light and thought have no physicality about them. On the other end of the spectrum are those things that we perceive to have physicality such as our bodies. In truth, non-physicality and physicality are just qualities of our perceptions rather than being the inherent quality of the manifestation.

As previously stated, the human body is perceived as being a physical structure but is, in fact, devoid of physicality at the atomic level. If you and I lack physicality, where does the sense of "I" come from? We live our entire lives referring to "I" or variations of it, such as "my" "mine," or "me." What is this "I?" Your sense of "I" is just a thought. You have an awareness of your own existence. The thought "I" is the recognition of our own existence. The thought "I" is the like a name tag that is worn by awareness. However, this thought is not awareness. Rather, you are aware of it. It is like having a thought of a car. The thought of a car is not the car; it just references it.

When your sense of "I" interacts with its other manifestations, it experiences contrast. To illustrate this, let us use a small child as an example. A child knows that it exists; he or she has an awareness of its own existence. The child is given two items of food to choose from them. The first item is a piece of candy and the second item is spinach. By sampling each of the food items, the child can experience contrast: The two items of food taste different from each other. This experience of contrast is what we know as experience.

The child's thought of "I" identifies with the experience of tasting the foods. For example, the "I" thought may identify with the thought "candy is more pleasurable than spinach." The "I" thought becomes a magnet that attracts other thoughts that are of the same quality. For example, the thought "I prefer candy" will attract other thoughts that are of similar quality such as "I want something sweet" or "Foods that are brightly colored are good."

Where do the thoughts that are attracted to the "I" thought come from? They come from what we sometimes refer to as the collective consciousness. Every thought that has ever been thought, or will be thought, exist already with the collective consciousness, also known as the Akashi Records. This is why it was stated earlier that you do not create or own your thoughts; rather, your "I" thought attracts them to it. The thought that is attracted are those thoughts that match the quality of thoughts that you have previously attracted. The child who had the thought "I like candy" will attract other thoughts that are consistent with that thought.

No thought has inherent power of its own. Any power that a thought possess is derived from the attention that we give it. If we remove our attention from a thought, it will lose its potency. When we give a great amount of attention to a thought, that thought becomes a belief. A belief is very powerful because it becomes a filter to how we experience life. If a person develops the belief that people cannot be trusted, that person will experience every interaction that they have as something they need to be suspect of. When we give a great deal of our attention to a belief, it becomes a conviction. Our convictions are so powerful that some people will kill themselves or others because of it.

Do-It-Yourself Energy Experiment:

The reason why the practice of meditation has to withstand the test of time is because it addresses a timeless problem, getting caught up in our thoughts. As stated before, the meaning of our experiences is not inherent in the experience. Instead, all meaning comes from the thoughts that we have of our experience. The practice of meditation and non-judgment are effective ways for reconditioning our mind. For most of us, our socialization has taught us to identify with our thoughts. Mediation and non-judgment train our attention so that we can be aware of our thoughts but not get involved with them.

The following exercise can be used to discover your core beliefs. Discovering your core beliefs is fundamental to making changes in your life.

1. The first step is to think of an ongoing challenge that you are experiencing in your life. My example will be: I am afraid of public speaking.
2. My next step is to start a line of inquiry using the phrase "What would be so bad if..." So my first question would be "What would be so bad about public speaking?"
3. My answer to that question would be "I might make a mistake or get nervous."

4. I would then use my response and rephrase the question: "What would be so bad if I made a mistake or was nervous?"

5. My response to that would be "People would think less of me."

6. I would continue to repeat this question by asking: "What would be so bad if people felt less of me?"
My answer to that would be "I would feel like I am unlovable."

7. Keep going through this line of questioning until you are unable to any further. When you have reached this point, you will have identified your subconscious belief. At the conscious level, I am aware of the fear of public speaking; however, the core belief behind that belief is "I feel like I am unlovable."

In the previous topic, we explored thoughts and beliefs. At your purest essence, you are devoid of a sense of ego or personal identity. That which we refer to as ego and personal identity are also thoughts and perceptions that we have of ourselves. Both ego and personality are like garments that your essential truth wears to experience the world. If you had no sense of "I," you could not have any sense of experience.

Ego is just a form of thought; however, it is the most powerful thought that we have regarding our level of conviction that we have for it. Your sense of identity is just a belief system. If you change your beliefs about yourself, you can change your identity. By learning how to create distance between yourself and your thoughts, you can reconfigure your mind so that you diminish our sense of identification with the ego and your sense of identity.

The following are some simple exercises, which with practice, can lead you to challenge your perceptions of who you are. Note: These exercises need to be continuously practiced to break through your conditioning and the belief systems that you have of yourself. The purpose of this exercise is to challenge your beliefs as to the nature of that which you refer to as "I."

1. Sit down, make yourself comfortable, and closed eyes.
2. Place your focus on your breathing.
3. When you feel relaxed, take note of any thoughts that you may be having. You can take note of thoughts because you are aware of them.
4. Now try to locate the "you" that is aware of thought. The "you" that I am referring to is that which each one of us calls "I."

Where is this "I" located, the one that is aware of thought? What are the qualities of this "I"? Is it big? Is it small? Does it have a color? Regardless of how you respond to these questions, you have not discovered the truth of who you are. Everything that you experience, including the answers to these questions, is also observed. Who you are at your most essential level cannot be experienced by you. That which you refer to as "I" is just another object being observed within your awareness. That which you refer to as "I" is a thought that you have learned to identify with. Who you are is that which observes all of experience!

Your sense of identity is just a set of beliefs that you have adopted for you to fit in with your family, culture, or society that you found yourself in.

As consciousness, you are the observer of all of experience, including your sense of "I" and your sense of identity.

Do-It-Yourself Energy Experiment:

The exercise described under this topic allows you to experience the letting go of your identification with your mind and body. It does take persistent practice, but the benefits are innumerable, including:
- Spending less time thinking and more time experiencing life.
- Developing a greater sense of connection with others.
- Transcending any critical thinking that you may have of yourself and others.
- Staying present
- Becoming more open to experience
- Transcending fears.
- Overcoming addictive behaviors.

Like everything else that we experience as being part of "reality," the subject of cause and effect is relative toward the level of awareness that it is being experienced from. Our everyday experience is found in the third-dimensional reality (the reality of physical form). It is in this reality that we can predict causation. If I throw a baseball at a window, the glass breaks. If I throw a ball up in the air, it will fall back to Earth. If I don't go to work, I will get fired. Most of what we understand of cause and effect is the result of Newtonian physics. Newtonian physics explains the laws that govern our world through the relationships between the motion of objects and the forces acting upon them. Much of our traditional scientific understanding came from Newtonian physics.

The advent of quantum physics shook the very foundation of Newtonian physics. At the atomic level, the ability to predict cause with effect was smashed. Researchers found solid particles acting like waves and waves acting like solid particles. They discovered that two particles could occupy the same space at the same time. They found that it is impossible to measure the velocity and direction of an atomic particle at the same time. In short, everything that we experience with a sense of certainty in our daily reality was lost at the quantum level.

Under the topic *That which lies beyond Ego and Personal Identity,* it was explained that which we refer to as "I" is just a thought of which we have identified with. How can we be sure that we know the correct relationship between cause and effect when most of the human species confuse the "I" thought with who they are? It is possible that which we take to be cause and effect is just our own dogmatic interpretation of what is really correlation?

Many religions have used cause and effect, known as karma, to maintain societal obedience. According to some religions, living in poverty is the result of past karma and that to change one's karma takes many life times. To have an impoverished population believe this makes it that much easier for the ruling party to maintain civil obedience.

Let's look at a different perspective of karma, as it relates to cause and effect. Every moment is a karmic moment, and every karmic moment lasts only as long as we allow it to. To better understand this, let us first look at the karmic cycle. The karmic cycle includes memory, desire, and action.

Let us say that you are walking on the street and you pass a restaurant. You detect a most pleasurable smell coming from it. The reason that you can identify that smell is because you have a memory of it from the past. The memory of the smell elicits the desire to taste the food. Your desire causes you to enter the restaurant and order the food, which is the action component of the karmic cycle. Once you have taken action by eating the food, you have completed the karmic cycle. The action of eating the food reinforces the existing memory of it, and the cycle continues.

Now let us look at a different scenario. Let us say that you are walking down the same street, and you smell the food coming from the restaurant. Instead of entering the restaurant, you walk past the restaurant. By walking past the food, you have changed your karma. The karmic cycle has been completed; however, your actions have created a new memory. The creation of a new memory creates a new desire and a new future.

If you look into last two scenarios more deeply, you may realize two important points. The first point is that karma can be changed in a moment. The second point is that your experience of karma had nothing to do with restaurant. In other words, it is not the circumstances in your life that influence your karma; rather, it is how you respond to them that determines it.

The most powerful thing that we can do to improve the quality of our lives is to develop greater awareness to the choices that we are making on a moment to moment basis. When we become conscious of our decision making, we become a conscious participant to the workings of the entire universe. When we become conscious decision makers, we enhance the quality of our lives and of all those around us.

Freedom is a universally desired by all living beings. Everyone wants to live a life free from restrictions or unpleasant conditions. The challenge for most of humanity is that the pursuit of freedom has its focus on the external world while ignoring the inner world. Imagine a person who is experiencing financial distress and is struggling just to make ends meet. This person does not experience the feeling of freedom because they are focusing on all the lack that exists in their lives.

Now suppose that this person's financial situation changes for the better. They start a business that becomes very successful, and they enjoy a dramatic change in income. This person now experiences numerous opportunities to enjoy themselves because of their success, which was nonexistent in the past. This person now enjoys a sense of freedom that they never had before.

While this person is enjoying their new life, they discover that a dear friend or family member has been diagnosed with cancer or some other life threatening disease. All of the sudden, the sense of freedom that this person was enjoying evaporates from their lives.

Because of our socialization and conditioning, we have come to be stimulus-response beings whose sense of freedom is dependent upon on whether or not the conditions of our life are aligned with our expectations. When the conditions of our life are aligned with our deepest desires, we experience a sense of freedom. However, this sense of freedom is impermanent. The nature of life is constant change. Any sense of freedom will last only as long as our conditions remain unchanged.

For most people, a sense of freedom comes about when they can escape from a situation that they find aversive. True freedom arises when we can experience a sense of peace regardless of the conditions that we experience.

Regardless of what we experience, no experience can enslave us or take away our freedom. From the perspective of higher consciousness, all of experience is ultimately a projection of pure consciousness. Everything that we experience, including our sense of being a person, and the thought of freedom, is just a potentiality that is being expressed by the greater consciousness.

The term "duality" means "two," while the term "non-duality" means "not two." The human species overwhelmingly experiences life from a dualistic perspective. "Us and them," "mine and yours," "good and bad," and "big and small," are all examples of dualism.

For most of the scientific age, the mind was viewed as separate from the body. It was only toward the modern age of science that the separation between mind and body began to dissolve. Research demonstrated that activity in the brain can affect the body, while activity in the body can affect the mind. At the same time, it is normal for people to experience the activity and functions of the mind as being separate from those of the body.

If you are worried our making your mortgage payment, most likely you are not giving thought to your body. If you just broke your arm, you most likely will not give attention to thoughts as they arise and fade in your consciousness. Both of these examples are legitimate perspectives of the mind-body relationship. To say that mind and body are separate from each other is a dualistic perspective. By saying that the mind body relationship is neither separate nor one is a nondual perspective.

The problems caused by concepts, as we discussed previously, extend to teachings of non-duality. Many teachers of non-duality treat it as something separate from duality, which is a dualistic perspective. A deeper look reveals that duality is found in non-duality and non-duality is found in duality.

While pure consciousness is one, its manifested expressions are infinite in their variety. Everything that we experience is a manifestation of pure consciousness. As limitless are the manifestations of pure consciousness are, every manifestation is pure consciousness at its most fundamental level. We can illustrate this by using a television set. Digital waves are filled with information that has been broken down. These waves are picked-up by the television, and their information is unscrambled. The image that we see on the television screen is formed by the numerous pixels that contain the recombined information. Our brains combine the information from the pixels to create an image that we recognize.

While the original digital wave could be considered non-dual, the infinite images that appear on the screen appear to be dualistic. The image of a can of cola is seen as being separate from the image of the person that is drinking it. In this manner, duality is found in non-duality as the television images are a function of the digital wave. Since the digital wave is found within the images on the screen, non-duality is found in duality.

Conclusion

If you put on a pair of red tinted sunglasses, everything that you see will appear red. If you put on a pair of green tinted sunglasses, everything that you see will appear green. The perspective that you experience wearing sunglasses is of little consequence to you because you know that your perspective is being distorted by the colored lenses. But what if you were born with your tinted sunglasses on? Given that you would not have had the opportunity to experience the world with them off, you would believe that your perspective of the world was accurate.

Every person is looking to understand something. Some people are looking to understand how they can improve themselves through self-help programs. Some people are looking to understand how they can improve their finances. There are scientist that are looking to understand the nature of black holes and outer space, and there are researchers that are looking to understand how certain biological organisms are able to fight of cancer.

Regardless of what we are seeking to understand, history has shown that we have neglected to try to understand the nature of who we are. How can we understand anything if we do not first understand ourselves. As long as we do not understand the nature of who we are, our efforts to understand the subject of our interest will be like the infant born with tinted sunglasses on.

As stated in the introduction, the purpose of this book is provide the reader with a different perspective, a perspective that is drastically different from our conventional thinking. This perspective is drastically different because it goes against everything that we were taught to believe.

A paradigm shift is a fundamental change in how we view the world. This change can occur at an individual or societal level. Examples of famous paradigm shifts in history include the view that the Earth is round, not flat, that the Earth revolves around the sun, that space-time is not fixed or objective, or the discovery of quantum mechanics. Each of these paradigm shifts were treated as "fringe" ideas that met much resistance. The gradual acceptance of these paradigm shifts eventually led to their widespread acceptance. As life changing as paradigm shifts have been on our lives, no paradigm shift has ever challenged the nature of who we are as human beings. As long as we view ourselves as being separate from the rest of life, we will engage in a mindset that is dominated by the beliefs that exploiting our planet and other people is justified in the name of progress, religion, or political expediency.

Every challenge that we face, both individually and collectively, is due to our inability to identify with others and our own fears of scarcity. The only reason why exploitation of others and the planet exists is because of our lack of compassion and our need to put our self-interest first. We lack compassion for others because we are unable to connect with ourselves. We place our self-interest first because we feel insignificant unless we can express overt power. That we, as a species, have difficulty identifying with others, or overcoming our self-interest, is not an accident. As we discussed in this book, we are all tapping into the collective consciousness. Nothing in life is eternal, except for life itself. Every time we take on a new perspective, we are contributing to the changing of the collective consciousness.

Consciousness is dynamic and ever changing. What fuels that change is the input that we give it through our thoughts. The evolution of consciousness starts with the evolution of thought within the individual.

Being able to experience yourself as multidimensional beings changes both you and the rest of humanity. With thoughtful self-inquiry, how can we dispute that we are part of a greater awareness while simultaneously being a physical being. If you apply what you have learned from this book with an open mind, and a persistent but patient attitude, you will be on the vanguard of a consciousness revolution.